Alan Posener

It's a Dog's Life

Two stories

Ernst Klett Schulbuchverlag
Stuttgart Düsseldorf Berlin Leipzig

Gedruckt auf Recyclingpapier,
hergestellt aus 100 % Altpapier.

1. Auflage 1 6 5 4 3 2 | 1999 98 97 96 95

Alle Drucke dieser Auflage können im Unterricht nebeneinander benutzt werden, sie sind untereinander unverändert. Die letzte Zahl bezeichnet das Jahr dieses Druckes.

Umschlag und Zeichnungen: Christian Gutendorf.
Satz: Setzerei Lihs, Ludwigsburg.
Druck: Röck, Weinsberg. Printed in Germany.
ISBN 3-12-571190-8

Contents

Jenny's dog

One: First day of the holidays

"Wake up, Jenny, wake up!"

"Mmmmm?"

"Wake up! It's nine o'clock! The sun is shining. Breakfast is . . ."

"Nine o'clock?" Jenny Jacobs sits up. Jenny's brother Toby is sitting on her bed. "Nine o'clock, Toby? It's time for school! We're late!"

Toby laughs. Then Jenny remembers. No school today. Today is the first day of the summer holidays. Jenny hits Toby with a pillow. Toby gets his pillow and hits Jenny. "Ow!" "Gotcha!" "Woof!"

Woof?

Monty is Jenny's dog. He sleeps under Jenny's bed every night. But now he isn't asleep – he wants to play, too. Of course Monty helps Jenny. She is his best friend. Monty pulls Toby's pyjama leg.

"Hey, stop it, Monty!" shouts Toby. "That's not fair!"

9	*summer* [ˈsʌmə]	Sommer
9	*to hit*	schlagen, treffen
10	*pillow*	Kopfkissen
10	*ow!* [aʊ]	Au!
11	*gotcha!* [ˈgɒtʃə]	Treffer!
11	*woof!* [wʊf]	Wuff!
16	*pyjama* [pəˈdʒɑːmə]	Schlafanzug, Pyjama
16	*leg*	Bein
17	*fair*	fair, gerecht

The door opens. "What's all this?" It's Mr Jacobs. "Stop that noise now, you two! Breakfast is ready – bacon and eggs. Oh dear, look at your room – what a mess! And we're going away today. Kids! Kids!!" Mr Jacobs goes back to the kitchen.

"Sorry, Dad!" calls Jenny. Then she puts on her jeans and a blouse.

The Jacobs family – Mr and Mrs Jacobs, Jenny and Toby – are going to Germany by car.

The Jacobses live in Sedgefield, a small town in England. Can you find it? Sedgefield has a twin town in Germany: Hamminkeln. This is how you get from Sedgefield to Hamminkeln:

From Sedgefield to Stockton. From Stockton to York on the A19. From York to Hull. Then by car ferry from Hull to Rotterdam, in Holland. You can sleep on the ferry. Then through Holland and into Germany.

It's a long trip. Jenny's first trip outside Britain.

"Holidays in Germany – wow!" says Jenny.

"A night on the car ferry – super!" says Toby. "Hey, Jenny, is there a good beach at Hamminkeln?"

"Don't be silly. Hamminkeln isn't at the seaside."

"Oh."

4	*kid*	Kind, Kleine(r)
8	*Germany* ['dʒɜ:mənɪ]	Deutschland
10	*twin town*	Partnerstadt
14	*A19*	eine größere Landstraße (vgl. Bundesstraße)
14	*ferry*	Fähre
15	*Holland*	Holland, die Niederlande
17	*trip*	Reise

Two: What about Monty?

Time to go! The family's bags are in the car. The car is ready and clean. The children's room is clean. (Well . . .) Mrs Jacobs has got the car keys. Mr Jacobs is looking for the house keys. ("They must be here somewhere . . .") Toby has got his walkman. Jenny has got Monty.

Mr Jacobs is still looking for the house keys. "The children can help you, dear," says Mrs Jacobs. "When you find the keys, bring them to Mrs Coates next door. And I can take Monty to the kennels in Bradbury."

Toby is listening to his walkman. He can't hear. But Jenny can. She looks at her mother. "Kennels? Kennels?? what do you mean? Monty's coming with us. He wants to see Germany, too!"

"I'm sorry, Jenny," says her mother. "We can't take Monty. If he goes out of Britain, we can't bring him back. They have rabies in Germany. People don't want rabies to come to Britain. So we can't take Monty. It's a very nice kennels, Jenny. And it's only three weeks."

"Only three weeks! Three weeks without my best friend! Oh, Monty!" Jenny wants to cry. She runs into the house and upstairs to her room.

"What's the matter with Jenny?" says Toby.

"I've got the keys!" says Mr Jacobs. "What's the matter with Jenny?"

"What's the matter with Jenny?" thinks Monty.

4	*somewhere*	irgendwo
9	*kennels*	Hundepension, Tierheim
16	*rabies* [ˈreɪbiːz]	Tollwut

Jenny looks out of her window. Monty is getting into the car. He is wagging his tail. He doesn't know about the kennels.

Three: The ferry

The car comes back – without Monty. Mr Jacobs and Toby get in.

"Come on, Jenny," says Mrs Jacobs. "Monty is OK. Mrs Taylor at the kennels is very nice. Everything is very clean. Perhaps Monty can find some friends there. Get in the car, we're late."

Jenny gets into the car. "Do you want to listen to my walkman?" asks Toby. And Mr Jacobs says, "Look, here's a nice sweet for you."

But Jenny doesn't want a walkman or a sweet. She wants her dog. She looks out of the window. But she doesn't see the road, the houses, and the other cars. She only sees Monty's face.

Mrs Jacobs drives to York. They have a cup of tea there. Then Mr Jacobs drives to Hull. There are signs: CAR FERRY. Lots of cars are waiting at the harbour. Soon they can drive right into the big ship.

Mr and Mrs Jacobs, Toby and Jenny get out of the car and go on deck. It is windy. Jenny says, "My coat is in the car. Can I go

2	*to wag his/her tail* [wæg]	mit dem Schwanz wedeln
3	*without*	ohne
17	*harbour* [ˈhɑːbə]	Hafen
18	*ship*	Schiff
20	*(on) deck*	(auf) Deck

and get it?" "OK," says Mrs Jacobs. "But hurry up! The ferry is leaving soon." "And bring my walkman with you!" calls Toby.

The ferry hoots. Then again. Now it is leaving the harbour. Toby jumps up and down – it is so exciting! Mr Jacobs shows Toby the sea, boats and ships in the harbour, a crane . . . There – someone is waving. Waving goodbye. A little girl, all alone. "Look! There's Jenny!" says Toby. "Don't be silly!" says Mr Jacobs. "Jenny is here on the . . ." Then he sees the girl. "But, but, but . . ." says Mr Jacobs. "Jenny!" cries Mrs Jacobs. The girl is still waving. But the ship is out of the harbour now, and the girl is far away and very small.

Four: A dog alone

In the kennels, Monty is waiting for his family. They must come soon. It's late. Time for supper. When Monty thinks of supper, he wags his tail. Why don't the Jacobses come back? They always come back for supper when they go away. They can't leave him here alone! Where is his friend Jenny? Who are all these other dogs? Why are they barking and crying? Why are they all in cages?

Monty is alone. He is afraid. He waits and waits. He barks and cries: don't forget me, Jenny! Jenny must hear him. She

1	*hurry up!* ['hʌrɪ ˌʌp]	beeil dich
3	*to hoot*	hupen, tuten
5	*boat*	Boot, Schiff
5	*crane*	Kran
6	*to wave*	winken
13	*supper* ['sʌpə]	Abendessen, Abendbrot
18	*cage* [keɪdʒ]	Käfig

must come and get him. Monty doesn't want to be alone at night.

A man comes and brings Monty his supper. But Monty doesn't wag his tail. He's hungry, but he can't eat. It's dark. And nobody comes.

Five: I'm coming, Monty!

Jenny is alone in Hull. It is a big town. Jenny wants to go to Bradbury and see Monty. She doesn't want to leave her friend alone in the kennels. She follows the signs: NORTH. She walks for an hour, but she is still in Hull. Jenny thinks, "Perhaps someone can take me to Bradbury." She stands on the side of the road with her thumb up. There are lots of cars on the road. Some cars hoot at Jenny, but they don't stop.

A truck stops. "Where are you going, young lady?" asks the driver.

"To Bradbury."

"Bradbury? Where's that?"

"It's . . . , well, it's in the north. On the M1 motorway."

"I can take you to York," says the truck driver. "Get in!"

8	*to follow*	folgen
8	*north*	(nach) Norden
10	*side*	Seite, Rand
11	*thumb* [θʌm]	Daumen
12	*to stop*	anhalten
13	*truck*	Lkw, Truck
13	*young* [jʌŋ]	jung
17	*motorway*	Autobahn (in GB)

The truck driver's name is Max. In York, Max buys Jenny a cup of tea and a sandwich. Jenny is very hungry. Max looks at her. "You know," he says, "it's dangerous for a young girl to hitch-hike all alone. It's dark outside." Jenny looks out of the window. It is dark. It's windy, and it's raining.

Jenny looks at the truck driver. "My parents are waiting for me," she says. "And my dog." Jenny starts to cry.

"Don't cry, young lady. Perhaps I can help you." Max stands up and goes away. People at other tables look at the little girl.

The truck driver comes back. A young woman is with him. She is wearing jeans and a cowboy shirt.

"You're lucky," Max tells Jenny. "My friend here is going to Newcastle on the M1. Bradbury is on the way. Jenny, this is Linda, the best truck driver in the North. Linda, this is Jenny. Please look after her."

"OK, Jenny, let's go," says Linda.

Jenny says goodbye to Max. Linda and Jenny walk outside.

"This . . . This is your truck?" asks Jenny. It's very big.

Six: We want to go back to England!

On the ferry, Mr and Mrs Jacobs run to the captain. "Stop the ship!" says Mr Jacobs. "We want to go back to England!"

"Why?" asks the captain. "Don't you like my ship?"

"It's a lovely ship," says Mr Jacobs. "But our little daughter is still in Hull. We must go back!"

3	*dangerous* ['deɪndʒərəs]	gefährlich
4	*to hitch-hike*	per Anhalter fahren
19	*captain* ['kæptɪn]	Kapitän
22	*daughter* ['dɔ:tə]	Tochter

"But why is your daughter in Hull? Why isn't she on the ferry?" asks the captain. "Doesn't *she* like my ship?"

"She likes your ship," says Toby. "But she likes her dog more."

The captain listens. Toby tells him about Monty and Jenny.

"So you see," says Mrs Jacobs, "we must go back. Please!"

"I'm sorry, I can't do that," says the captain. "I've got a hundred cars and trucks and four hundred passengers on this ferry. They want to be in Rotterdam tomorrow. But I can send a radio message to the police. The police can find your daughter. And tomorrow you can take the next ferry back to Hull."

The captain takes the Jacobses to the radio room. He sends a radio message to the police in Hull.

"There!" says the captain. "The police are looking everywhere in Hull for your daughter. She can't go very far."

The sea is dark. It's windy. Mr and Mrs Jacobs and Toby go to bed, but they can't sleep.

Seven: The runaway

In the kennels, Monty is still waiting. He is worried. Perhaps something is wrong with his family. With Jenny! He must help her! But how? He is in a cage. He can't get out. But he must get out! Monty barks and barks: I want to get out of this cage. I want to find Jenny! A man shouts, "Stop that noise!" A woman says, "It's the new dog. Give him some more to eat, Sam."

9 *tomorrow*	morgen
10 *message* ['mesɪdʒ]	Nachricht
18 *he is worried* ['wʌrɪd]	er macht sich Sorgen
19 *something*	(irgend)etwas

Monty has an idea. When Sam comes to Monty's cage, Monty is lying on the floor. Is he sleeping? Sam looks into the cage. Monty's supper is still there. Sam is worried. Is the new dog ill? He calls, "Here now, good boy! Come on, eat your supper now! Good boy, good ..." The dog is still lying on the floor. Now Sam is very worried. He opens the door of the cage with his key and comes in. He doesn't shut the door. Suddenly, Monty jumps up. He barks: GRRRUFF! Sam is afraid. "Help! Help, Mrs Taylor! Down, boy, down, g-g-g-good dog. He-help!" The other dogs are barking and laughing. Mrs Taylor calls, "What's the matter, Sam? Wait there. I'm coming!"

Monty doesn't wait. He jumps over Sam and runs through the open cage door. "Hey, you silly dog! What are you doing? Where are you going? Stop! Come back!" cries Mrs Taylor. But Monty doesn't stop. He runs through the kennels. Everywhere, dogs are jumping and barking in their cages: The gate is on the right! Be careful on the road! Good luck! Goodbye!

Monty runs out of the gate and onto the road. Careful! Cars hoot, drivers shout. Monty runs on the side of the road. Sam and Mrs Taylor run after him. But not for long. Soon Monty is alone. Where is his home? Monty can't read the signs on the road. But he listens to the wind. He looks at the stars and the moon. The wind, the moon and the stars tell him the way home. Monty runs through the night. He's happy now. I'm coming, Jenny!

2	*to lie*	liegen
16	*gate*	Tor
22	*star*	Stern
23	*moon*	Mond

Eight: A police message

It's warm in Linda's big truck. Outside, Jenny sees the lights of cars and other trucks. She is very tired. She thinks of Monty. Then she thinks of her mother and father and Toby. "Sorry, Mum. Sorry, Dad. Sorry, Toby," she says. Linda can't hear. She's listening to country music on her radio: "Old Shep", a song about a boy and his dog. Suddenly, the song stops. A man says, "We have a police message. The police are looking for a young girl, Jennifer Jacobs. Jennifer is eleven years old. She has got grey eyes and brown hair. She is wearing a blue coat, blue jeans and a white blouse. The police think Jennifer is going to Sedgefield or Bradbury. If you see Jennifer, please call the police. And here is a message for Jennifer. Are you listening, Jennifer? Your parents are very worried, but they are not angry. Please call the police. This is a police message. Thank you."

Linda looks at Jenny. But Jenny is asleep. Linda says, "Jenny! Jenny, wake up ..."

"Mmmmh? Time for school? Oh no, Mum, I ... Oh!"

"Jenny, why are you running away? Is that right? Your parents are worried."

"How do you know?" asks Jenny.

"A police message on the radio. You're not going home, you're running away. I can't help you if you do something wrong, you know. I must call the police."

"No, don't call the police. I must see Monty. My parents are

2	*tired* ['taɪəd]	müde, erschöpft
5	*country music* ['kʌntrɪ]	Country-Musik
9	*eye* [aɪ]	Auge
9	*hair*	Haar, Haare

worried about me. But I'm worried about Monty. He's all alone, and ..."

"Wait, wait, wait! Tell me your story from the beginning. Who's Monty? And where are your parents? And why are you running away?"

Jenny tells Linda her story. The truck is still driving through the night. They see a sign: "Bradbury 22." Linda thinks. Then she says, "Listen, Jenny. We can drive to the kennels and see Monty. But then we must go to the police. OK?"

Jenny looks at Linda. "OK. And ..."

"What?"

"Thanks."

Chapter nine: Be careful, Monty!

Monty runs through the night. The lights of cars and trucks go by on the road. Some drivers hoot at Monty. In their cars they say, "Silly dog. Why isn't he at home? This road is dangerous."

More lights. This time it's a van. The driver hoots at Monty, the van goes by. Then it stops. Monty sees the red lights.

Two men get out of the van and look at Monty.

The two men catch stray dogs and stray cats: dogs and cats without a home. But the men don't take these stray dogs and

3	*beginning*	Anfang, Beginn
13	*to go by*	vorbeigehen, vorbeifahren
19	*to catch*	fangen, einfangen
19	*stray dog/cat* [streɪ]	streunende(r) Hund/Katze

cats to the police or to a pets' home. They sell them to a laboratory for tests and experiments. After some days or weeks, the animals are dead. And the laboratory must have new animals. It's a good job for the two men – good money.

"We're lucky," says one of the men. "He's a nice dog. Big! We can get a hundred pounds for him. Catch him, Fred!"

"Why me? You're right, he is big. You catch him, Brian!"

"OK, you and me. But you go first."

"No, you go first."

Monty looks at the two men. He doesn't understand them. Are they friends? He wags his tail.

"Look, he's wagging his tail," says Brian. "This is easy. Trick nineteen."

Brian fetches some dog food from the van. "Good dog! Come here, boy! Mmmmmm – yum-yum-yum! Suppertime!" calls Fred. He's right, thinks Monty. It is suppertime. Monty is very hungry. He goes to the van. The food looks good. Monty doesn't see Fred with the sack and the big stick.

Ten: Trick nineteen-and-a-half

"Here we are!" shouts Jenny. Linda stops the truck near a sign: TAYLOR'S HAPPY DOG KENNELS – GIVE YOUR DOG A HOLIDAY! Linda and Jenny walk to the gate. Dogs are

1	*laboratory* [lə'bɒrətrɪ]	Labor
2	*experiment* [ɪk'sperɪmənt]	Versuch, Experiment
3	*animal* ['ænɪməl]	Tier
3	*dead* [ded]	tot
4	*money* ['mʌnɪ]	Geld
18	*sack*	Sack

barking, and Sam is running from cage to cage. “Shhhh! Stop that noise now! Go to sleep!”

Linda looks at the sign again. “These are happy dogs? This is a dog holiday?” she says. Mrs Taylor comes to the gate. “What is it now?” she asks. Then she sees the truck. “Oh, are you the people with the dog food? You’re very late.”

“No, Mrs Taylor. I’m Jenny – Jennifer Jacobs. I want to see my dog. Is he OK?”

“Your dog? Hmmmph! That silly animal!” Mrs Taylor is very angry.

“Monty isn’t silly, Mrs Taylor. He’s my best friend. Can I see him now, please?”

“No, you can’t see him. Your dog isn’t here. He’s gone.”

“Gone?” asks Linda. “What do you mean?”

“I mean gone. I’m sorry, Jennifer. I’m sorry and I’m worried. That road is dangerous. And the silly – sorry, dear – the poor dog is all alone out there. And we can’t find him in the dark. I’ve no idea where he is.”

“But I know where he’s going!” says Jenny. “He’s going home – to our house in Sedgefield! Please take me to Sedgefield, Linda! Please! It’s not far. I know Monty is there! We must find him, and then we can go to the police.”

“Police?” says Mrs Taylor. “What … ?”

But Jenny and Linda are running to the big truck.

Linda drives, and Jenny looks out of the window. Is that a dog? No, silly, it’s a man on a bike. Jenny sees a van at the side of the road. Jenny isn’t looking for a van, she’s looking for a dog. But wait! What are those two men doing? They are fighting with a big dog. One of the men has got a sack and a stick. “Stop!” shouts Jenny. “They’ve got Monty!”

It's not easy to stop the big truck, and when they get out of the truck, Linda and Jenny can only see the lights of the van. They can't see the two men and Monty. "Hurry up!" says Jenny. "We mustn't come too late!"

"I'm coming, I'm coming!" says Linda. "Wait a minute. Now is the time for a trick." She fetches a flashlight from the truck. Then Linda and Jenny run to the van.

The two men are still fighting with Monty. Fred has got his arms round Monty, Brian has got the sack open in one hand and the big stick in the other hand. "Stop! Police!" shouts Linda. She shines the flashlight into the two men's eyes. They can't see. Brian pulls the sack over Fred's head. "Gotcha, you silly dog!" he shouts. Then he hits Fred with the stick: "Take that! Hey Fred, the police – let's go !" But Fred is sitting on the ground with his head in his hands. "Ow! Ow!" he cries. "Oh, oh!" says Brian and runs to the van. But Monty pulls his trouser leg. Brian's trousers come down and he falls on his face. Monty stands on him and barks.

"Help! Police! I'm dead!" shouts Brian. "Ow! my head!" says Fred.

Jenny runs to Monty and puts her arms round him: "Oh, Monty!" she says. Monty wags his tail and barks.

But what's that noise? It comes from the van. Jenny opens the back door. The van is full of dogs and cats in little cages. They are barking and meowing. "Oh no! The poor animals!" says Jenny. "We must help them. But how? Can you drive this

6	*flashlight*	Taschenlampe
15	*ground* [graʊnd]	Boden, Erde
25	*to meow* [mɪˈaʊ]	miauen

van to the police station, Linda?" "Easy. But what about these two animal lovers here? What can we do with them?"

"You can let us go," says Brian.

"Ow, my head!" says Fred.

"You're coming with us to the police," says Linda. "Get in the back of the van."

"No," says Brian. Monty barks: GRRUFF! Linda picks up the stick. Brian looks at Monty, Linda, and the stick. "OK," he says. "Can I pull up my trousers, please?"

Eleven: Home again – A day later

"Wake up, Jenny, wake up!"

"Mmmmh?"

"It's eleven o'clock. The sun's shining, breakfast is ready, and I think your parents are coming," says Linda.

"Woof!" says Monty under the bed. Jenny jumps out of bed and runs to the window. Her mother, father and brother are getting out of the car. Jenny puts on her jeans and her blouse and runs downstairs.

Mr and Mrs Jacobs go to the front door of their house. Mr Jacobs is very angry. His face is white. Then the door opens. Jenny and Monty are standing there with Linda. Jenny is afraid. But Monty wags his tail. Now the family is together again! Good! "Mum, Dad ... I'm so sorry!" says Jenny. And she is.

1 *police station*	Polizeirevier
2 *lover* ['lʌvə]	Liebhaber

Mr and Mrs Jacobs can see that. Mr Jacobs forgets that he is angry. He puts his arms round his daughter.

Then Monty tells Mr and Mrs Jacobs and Toby all about the kennels, Sam, the van and the two men, the sack, the big stick and the flashlight. He barks and barks. "Monty! Stop that noise!" shouts Mrs Jacobs. She looks at Linda. "You must be Linda. The police told us ... Well, thank you."

"That's all right, Mrs Jacobs. Look – I've got breakfast for us all in the kitchen. Nice hot tea and bacon and eggs and toast. Come in and welcome home!"

So the Jacobses have breakfast. They are all very hungry. Jenny and Linda tell their story. Mr Jacobs looks at his daughter. He isn't angry now. "Hmmm," he says. "It's all right now. But Jenny – don't run away again." And then he says, "Well then, it's holidays in England again. We can drive to the seaside."

"The seaside – yippee!" shouts Toby.

"Woof!" says Monty.

"Yes, that's a good idea," says Mrs Jacobs. "There's a nice hotel in Whitby. They like dogs, so we can take Monty with us."

"And Queenie," says Jenny.

"Who? Do you mean Linda?" asks Toby.

"No – Queenie. Monty's new friend. From the van, you see. She hasn't got a home. She's a lovely dog, Mum, very small, and clean, and – well, Monty likes her, and ..."

"Where is this Queenie?" asks Mrs Jacobs. "Not in the house?"

7	*the police told us* [təʊld]	die Polizei hat uns erzählt
8	*that's all right*	das geht schon in Ordnung
10	*welcome*	willkommen

"Well, yes. She's upstairs. Under Toby's bed," says Jenny.

"Listen, we can't have two dogs," says Mr Jacobs, but Toby says, "Why not? Jenny has got Monty. And Queenie can be my dog." He calls, "Queenie! Queenie!" Queenie runs downstairs and into the kitchen. Toby takes her into his arms. "She's lovely!" he says. "Can I keep her, Mum, Dad? Please? Please?!"

Monty and Queenie say please, too. They bark and bark. Linda and Jenny laugh.

Mr Coates next door says, "That Jacobs family – they're nice people, but oh, that noise!"

Linda says, "I must go now. My boss is waiting. Goodbye, Mr and Mrs Jacobs. Goodbye Jenny – and Monty. And listen: don't run away again, OK?"

"OK. Thank you Linda – goodbye."

Jenny and Monty watch. The big truck drives away. Toby is playing with Queenie, Mrs Jacobs is ringing up the hotel in Whitby, Mr Jacobs is washing up. Linda waves again. "Goodbye!" calls Jenny.

"Woof!" says Monty.

Two dogs at the seaside

One: Fun in Whitby

It's 10 o'clock on Saturday morning. Time to go to Whitby! The family's bags are in the car. The car is ready and clean. The children's room is ... well, *you* know. Mrs Jacobs has got the car keys, and Mr Jacobs has got the house keys ... has he? ("They are here somewhere, I know ...") Jenny has got Toby's walkman. Toby is in the car with Queenie and Monty. "Come on!" shouts Toby. "Woof! Woof!" bark the dogs.

Mrs Coates lives next door. She looks out of her window. "Goodbye!" she calls. "Oh, Mr Jacobs! I've got your house keys, remember?" Jenny gets into the car, then Mr and Mrs Jacobs get in. "Goodbye, Mrs Coates!" they call. "Woof! woof!" Vrrrroom! "Well, they're gone," says Mrs Coates. "Mmmmm," says Mr Coates. "Isn't it quiet? Lovely!"

It's not far from Sedgefield to Whitby. (Can you find the way?) From Sedgefield to Middlesbrough on the A 177, then on the A 174 to the sea. Marske-by-the-Sea, Saltburn-by-the-Sea, Sandsend – Whitby. In the car, the Jacobses play "Twenty Questions". Monty and Queenie bark at the dogs in other cars. They all have fun.

The hotel is near the sea. Mrs Jacobs stops the car. "Who's first at the sea?" shouts Jenny. She runs to the beach. Who's first? Monty, of course. Then Queenie. Then Jenny, then Toby.

12 *vrrrooom!* [vru:m]
13 *quiet* [ˈkwaɪət] ruhig

"Hey!" shouts Mrs Jacobs. "What about your bags? What about lunch? Oh, those kids!" Then she laughs.

The sun is shining, the sea is blue. Jenny takes off her shoes and her jeans and runs into the sea with Monty and Queenie. Then she runs out again. Brrrr! It's cold!

"I know!" says Jenny. "Let's play cricket!"

"Good idea!" says Toby. He runs back to the hotel and fetches his cricket bat and a ball. Jenny makes a wicket with four sticks. (Can you play cricket? It's fun – a great game for the beach.)

Jenny throws the ball. Toby hits it with the bat. The dogs run to get the ball and bring it back to Jenny. A boy is sitting near them all alone. He watches the game. Sometimes he laughs at the dogs.

When Jenny hits the wicket with the ball Toby is "out". Now it's Toby's turn to throw and Jenny gets the bat. Toby throws the ball . . . Jenny hits it . . . Wow! The ball goes up, up, up. "Woof! Woof!" bark the dogs. They can't see the ball because the sun is shining. Now it's coming down. "Help!" shouts Toby and puts his arms over his head. "Gotcha!" says a voice. "You're out!" It's the boy. He's got the cricket ball in his hands.

"I'm not out!" shouts Jenny. "You're not in the game!" But Toby says, "Do you want to play with us? What's your name?"

The boy's name is Dennis Owen. He is eleven years old, like Jenny. "I'm here with my mother," he tells Jenny and Toby.

6	*cricket* ['krɪkɪt]	Cricket
8	*bat*	Schläger (beim Cricket)
8	*wicket*	Pfostentor beim Cricket
17	*wow!* [waʊ]	Ausruf des Erstaunens

Dennis shows Jenny and Toby his mother. She is sitting on the beach not very far away. She's reading a book and drinking tea. Dennis lives alone with his mother. He hasn't got a brother or sister. "No sister? You're lucky!" says Toby. But Dennis says, "It's terrible when you're on holiday all alone." "Well, then," says Jenny. "You can play with us. But I'm not out yet, OK?"

"OK!" laughs Dennis.

But soon Dennis hits the wicket and Jenny is out. Dennis takes the bat. Jenny throws the ball and Dennis hits it – up, up, up – down, down, down . . . zing! "Help!" shouts Toby. "Oh, oh!" says Jenny. The ball is in Mrs Owen's cup of tea! The cup breaks, and Mrs Owen is very wet. Monty and Queenie run to get the ball. They jump over Mrs Owen and bark. They are full of sand, and now Mrs Owen has got sand in her hair, her eyes, her blouse, and her book, and tea and sand on her skirt. She is very angry. "Come here, Dennis!" she shouts. "You can't play those silly games with those silly children! And you two! Take those terrible dogs away from here!"

"But Mum . . ." says Dennis.

"We're very sorry . . ." says Jenny.

"Woof!" says Monty.

But Mrs Owen doesn't listen. "Come along, Dennis," she says. "We're going. Oh, those terrible dogs!"

10 *zing!* [zɪŋ]

Two: Those terrible dogs again …

In the evening, the Jacobses have supper in the hotel dining-room. The hotel manager likes dogs, so Monty and Queenie can sit under the table. A boy and his mother are sitting at the next table. "Look, Mum and Dad, it's our friend Dennis!" says Toby. "Hello, Dennis, good evening Mrs Owen," says Jenny. "Hello!" laughs Dennis. But Mrs Owen says, "Hmmmph!"

"Mum," says Dennis. "I don't like my supper. You know I don't eat steak." It's a very big steak, and very red.

"Don't be silly, Dennis. Steak is good for you. Do you want to stay so small? Now eat your steak. It's very good."

"If it's so good, you can eat it, Mum!"

"Dennis!"

Mrs Owen eats her steak and takes out a map. She wants to go for a long walk on the moors the next day. She looks at the map. Dennis cuts his steak into two pieces. "Pssst! Monty! Queenie! Here – mmmmm, lovely steak!"

Monty and Queenie look at the pieces of steak in Dennis's hand. They wag their tails. Then they look at Mrs Jacobs: can we have the nice steak? Good dogs! But suddenly, a big white dog runs up to Dennis, takes the two pieces of steak out of his hands and runs away to another table. Oh no! Monty and Queenie are very angry. They bark at the white dog: Bring that steak back here! The white dog barks: Come and get it! Monty

2	*manager*	*hier:* Direktor
9	*steak* [steɪk]	Steak
15	*moor(s)* [mʊə(z)]	Moor

and Queenie jump up and run after the white dog. He runs away with the pieces of steak in his mouth. The dogs run under tables and chairs, through people's legs, all round the dining room. Monty and Queenie bark, and the white dog wags his tail: What a great game!

"Queenie!" shouts Toby. "Monty!" shouts Jenny. "Bonzo! Come here!" shout some people at another table. Everywhere people are shouting or laughing at the dogs. What a noise! Then the dogs run out of the door.

The hotel manager comes into the dining room. "What's the matter?" he says. Mrs Owen is very angry. She calls the hotel manager to her table. "Those terrible dogs again!" she says. "Is this a hotel or a kennels? If those animals stay, I'm going!"

"Oh dear!" says the hotel manager. He looks at the Jacobses. "I'm sorry, Mr and Mrs Jacobs, but your dogs must stay in your rooms when they are in the hotel. We can't have animals in the dining-room."

"But ..." says Mr Jacobs.

"But ..." says Jenny.

"But Mum ..." says Dennis.

"I'm sorry," says the hotel manager.

Three: That silly brother! That terrible sister!

The next morning after breakfast, Mrs Owen goes on her long walk. "Can I stay here, Mum?" asks Dennis at breakfast. "I want to play with my new friends Jenny and Toby."

"Hmmm," says Dennis's mother. "But a walk is good for you, Dennis. Do you want to stay so small? And those Jacobs children, well ..."

"Please, Mum!"

"Well, I ..."

"Thanks, Mum!" And Dennis gives her a big kiss.

Dennis plays with Jenny and Toby on the beach. They play cricket and football, catch and hide-and-seek. They swim in the sea and come out blue with cold. For lunch they have a picnic on the beach: tea and sandwiches.

Dennis tells Jenny and Toby about himself. He lives with his mother in York. His father is in London. He's got a new wife.

"Poor Mum," says Dennis. "It's not easy for her."

"Poor you," says Jenny and holds his hand.

After lunch, Toby wants to play cricket again, but Dennis wants to visit Whitby harbour.

"Well, Jenny, what do you say?" asks Toby.

"Let's go to the harbour," says Jenny. Toby is very angry. His face is red. "Of course!" he shouts. "You always do what he wants! I'm your brother, don't forget!"

"You're silly, that's what you are!" says Jenny. "What do you mean – I always do what he wants?"

"You throw him easy balls when we play cricket, you pass the ball to him when we play football, you always catch him when we play catch and you find him when we play hide-and-seek. And now look, you're holding his hand!"

3	*kiss*	Kuß
5	*catch*	*Spiel:* Fangen, Nachlaufen
5	*hide-and-seek*	*Spiel:* Verstecken
9	*wife*	Ehefrau
20	*to pass* (the ball in football)	zuspielen, abgeben

"I'm not, silly!" Jenny puts her hands in the pockets of her jeans.

"Who's silly?"

"You are!"

"I'm not, you are!"

"Come on, Queenie!" says Toby. "Let's leave these two alone." And Toby walks off with his dog.

"That silly brother," says Jenny. "Oh, come on, Dennis, let's visit the harbour. Come on, Monty!"

"That terrible sister!" says Toby to Queenie. "You're lucky. You haven't got a sister."

Four: Alone on the moors

Toby walks and walks and walks – away from the beach, the sea, the town, onto the moors. He is angry and sad. "Sisters – huh!" he tells Queenie. "Jenny and her lover-boy Dennis!"

Toby walks and walks. He doesn't see the black clouds, he doesn't hear the wind. Soon it's dark. Time to go home! It's raining, too. "Oh dear, Queenie, we're late for supper!" says Toby. "And I think . . . I think we're lost. We must find the hotel. Queenie! Come back!"

1 *pocket*	Tasche (von einem Kleidungsstück)
13 *sad*	traurig
14 *huh!* [hə]	
15 *cloud* [klaʊd]	Wolke
16 *wind*	Wind

But Queenie hears something. She goes on. And soon Toby can hear it too – a voice far away. "Help! Help!" calls the voice. Queenie barks. The voice comes again, louder. "Help! I'm here! I can't walk!"

"I know that voice," says Toby. He shouts, "Hello! We're coming!" Now it's very dark, but soon Toby sees Mrs Owen. She is sitting on the ground and holding her foot. "I can't walk," she says again. "Can you help me?"

Toby wants to help Mrs Owen, but she's too heavy. She holds his arm and stands up, but then Mrs Owen and Toby fall down.

"Oh dear, oh dear!" cries Mrs Owen. "What can we do?"

"I can go back to the hotel and get help – if I can find the hotel," says Toby.

"No – no, don't go away!" says Mrs Owen. Then Toby has an idea. "Queenie! Queenie, run to the hotel – there's a good girl – run to the hotel and get help!"

Queenie looks at him and wags her tail. What does he want? She doesn't understand.

"Go on, Queenie! Go away! To the hotel! To Jenny! And Monty!" Monty! Now Queenie understands. She wags her tail, barks and runs away.

2	*help*	Hilfe
3	*louder* ['laʊdə]	lauter
7	*foot* [fʊt]	Fuß
9	*heavy* ['hevɪ]	schwer

Five: Dennis and Jenny

Dennis and Jenny visit the harbour and look at the ships and boats. They eat ice-cream at a snack bar. But Jenny isn't happy. "It's no fun without Toby," she says.

Toby! Monty wags his tail. He thinks about Toby and Queenie. He wags his tail some more and barks: Come on, you two! Let's find Toby and Queenie!

"What's the matter with Monty?" asks Dennis. "Hey – where is he going?" And Jenny calls, "Monty! It's time for supper! We must go back to the hotel! Come back, you silly dog!"

But Monty doesn't listen. And so Dennis and Jenny run after him. It's dark now and it's raining.

Suddenly, Monty stops and listens. Dennis and Jenny listen, too. Now they can hear something: a dog is barking somewhere. Monty barks – then the other dog barks again. "I know that voice!" says Jenny. "It's Queenie." And there she is! But where's Toby? Queenie barks: Follow me! Hurry up!

Monty, Dennis and Jenny run after her.

Six: First aid

Soon they can see Toby and Mrs Owen.

Dennis holds his mother's hand and Jenny looks at Mrs Owen's foot. "It's not broken," she says. Jenny and Dennis have

2	*ice-cream*	Eis, Eiskrem
	first aid	Erste Hilfe
20	*broken*	gebrochen

got the bag with their swimming things; Jenny takes out a towel and ties it round Mrs Owen's foot. "Ow!" says Mrs Owen. But now she can stand up when the children help her. But she can't walk.

"I've got an idea," says Toby. He takes the cricket bat out of the bag. Jenny and Toby hold one end of the bat, Dennis holds the other end. Mrs Owen sits on the bat and the children carry her. "Is it all right?" asks Mrs Owen. "You're so small, Dennis."

"Oh, Mum!" Dennis laughs.

But Mrs Owen is very heavy. And it's a long way to the hotel. The children carry Mrs Owen for ten minutes. Then Toby says, "I can't go on!"

Queenie looks at the children and Mrs Owen. She barks and runs away. She knows what she must do now.

Seven: Where are the children?

At the hotel, Mr and Mrs Jacobs are worried. Where are the children? Where are the dogs? Mr and Mrs Jacobs look for them on the beach and in the harbour – but they can't find them. Mrs Jacobs says, "Well, we must call the police." "Oh no, not again!" says Mr Jacobs.

Mr and Mrs Jacobs go to the hotel manager. He is talking on the telephone. "Yes ... Yes, that's right ... Mrs Owen ... O-W-E-N ... No, she's not my wife ... My name? ... Why do you ... Yes, yes, I see. My name's Blunt, B-L-U-N-T, and I'm the manager of the Sands Hotel. Mrs Owen is staying here and I'm

1 *swimming things*	Schwimmzeug, Schwimmsachen
1 *towel* ['taʊəl]	Handtuch

very worried because ... No, she isn't here now, that's why ... She's staying here, but she isn't here ... I think she's alone on the moors, and it's late, and I'm ..."

"Are you talking to the police?" says Mrs Jacobs.

"Shhh! I'm talking to the police!" says Mr Blunt. "Yes, I know you know you're the police, but ..."

"Our children are missing, too," says Mr Jacobs. "And Mrs Owen's son. And our dogs."

"Your dogs are missing? Good!" says Mr Blunt. "I mean: Oh dear, I'm so sorry. Poor dogs. What am I talking about?" he says into the telephone. "Oh, nothing, nothing ... I mean ... Look, please send somebody to my hotel, OK? And please hurry up!"

Mr Blunt puts down the telephone. "The moors are very dangerous when it's dark," he says.

Some minutes later, a police car arrives at the hotel. Two policemen get out. The hotel manager is waiting for them. One of the policemen looks at a piece of paper in his hand. "Mr Sands?" he says. "No, my name is Blunt." "Blunt? No, we're looking for Mr Sands, the hotel manager." "I'm the hotel manager, and my name's Sands – I mean Blunt. We're very worried about a lady and two – no, three children, and three – no, two dogs ..." "Children? Dogs?" The policeman looks at the piece of paper again. "That's funny. Is this the right hotel?"

Then Mrs Jacobs says, "Look!"

Queenie runs through the hotel door. She is wet and dirty. "Oh no!" cries Mr Blunt. "My nice, clean floor!" But

8	*son* [sʌn]	Sohn
9	*I mean*	ich meine natürlich
17	*policeman*	Polizist
26	*wet*	naß

Mrs Jacobs says, “This dog can help us. Queenie! Where are the children?” Queenie barks and runs out of the door. Mr and Mrs Jacobs follow her. The policemen get a flashlight and a walkie-talkie from their car and run after Mr and Mrs Jacobs. “Wait for me!” calls Mr Blunt. “Now, where’s my coat? And where’s my hat? And my umbrella. There! I’m ready! Oh – where is everybody?”

Mr and Mrs Jacobs and the two policemen soon find the three children and Mrs Owen with Monty. The policemen use their walkie-talkie and call an ambulance for Mrs Owen. “But what about Dennis?” says Mrs Owen when the ambulance comes.

“Don’t worry about me, Mum,” says Dennis.

“Dennis can have supper with us,” says Mr Jacobs.

“Supper? Good idea – I’m hungry!” says Toby.

“Can Dennis sleep in our room?” asks Jenny.

“Well, I . . .” says Mr Jacobs.

“Good idea!” says Toby. “We’re friends again, Dennis, OK?”

Eight: What a night!

Dennis’s mother must stay in hospital until the next day. Dennis is a bit sad. But not very sad, because after supper Mr Jacobs gets an old sleeping-bag from the car and says, “Well, Dennis, you can sleep on the sofa in the children’s room.”

4	*walkie-talkie*	Sprechfunkgerät
6	*umbrella* [ʌmˈbrelə]	Regenschirm
11	*ambulance* [ˈæmbjʊləns]	Krankenwagen
19	*hospital* [ˈhɒspɪtəl]	Krankenhaus
21	*sleeping bag*	Schlafsack

"Hooray!" shout Jenny and Toby.

Monty and Queenie wag their tails.

It's a great night. There's a TV in the children's room, so they watch TV until ten – a pop music special. Then Mr Jacobs comes in and says, "No more TV, please, time for bed!" So the children put on their pyjamas and have a great pillow fight. Then Mr Jacobs comes in again and says, "Shhh! It's eleven o'clock!" Jenny has some sweets, Dennis has some chocolate, and Toby has some lemonade and biscuits. So the three children have a midnight party on the floor. Monty and Queenie have some biscuits, too. The children talk and laugh. At twelve o'clock, somebody bangs on the wall. "Time for bed!" says Toby. Soon he is asleep. When Mrs Jacobs comes in at one o'clock, Toby and the dogs are asleep, but Dennis and Jenny are talking and listening to Toby's walkman together. "Now, you two," says Mrs Jacobs, "after a long day you must get some sleep."

"Yes Mum," says Jenny.

"OK, Mrs Jacobs," says Dennis.

And at two o'clock, Jenny and Dennis are asleep, too.

4	*pop music*	Popmusik
6	*pillow fight*	Kissenschlacht
10	*midnight* ['mɪdnaɪt]	Mitternacht
12	*to bang*	schlagen, heftig klopfen
14	*to be asleep*	schlafen
16	*sleep*	Schlaf

Nine: All's well that ends well

The next morning, Mrs Owen comes back from the hospital. She can walk with a stick and she has a big bandage on her foot. ("You're right, Jenny," she says, "it isn't broken.") The hotel manager is waiting for Mrs Owen with some red roses. Dennis and Mr Blunt bring Mrs Owen to the breakfast table. She says hello and thank you to everybody. "Call me Dorothy," she says. "Let's all have breakfast together. Come on, we can push these tables together. Well, I am hungry!"

Mr Blunt brings "the Sands Hotel super breakfast": cornflakes, bacon and eggs, sausages, chips, toast, butter and marmalade, and of course lots of tea.

"Ah!" says Mrs Owen. "Lovely!" Then she says, "One minute. Where are Monty and Queenie?"

Where are they? Upstairs of course, in the children's bedroom.

"But Mrs Owen ..." says Mr Blunt.

"Dorothy."

"But Dorothy, you know you ..."

"Yes, yes, I know. I'm sorry about that. But those dogs aren't terrible dogs. They're clever dogs. And I want to say thank you and give them something. Mr Blunt ..."

"Richard."

"Well, Richard, please bring me some more sausages from the kitchen. And Jenny ..."

But Jenny is already running upstairs. "Monty, Queenie! You lucky dogs! Time for your second breakfast!"

	all's well that ends well	Ende gut, alles gut
2	*bandage* ['bændɪdʒ]	Verband
20	*clever*	klug, intelligent

Ten: Goodbye

One week later it is time for Dennis and his mother to go back to York. The Jacobses and Mr Blunt take Dennis and Mrs Owen to the station.

Everyone is sad. Jenny cries a bit.

The train leaves the station. Dennis waves and shouts, "Goodbye, Jenny!" "Goodbye!" "Woof!"

Then the Jacobses go to the beach. It's a lovely day. The sky is blue, the sun is shining, it's warm. "Let's play cricket," says Mrs Jacobs. "Good idea!" says Mr Jacobs. But Jenny doesn't want to play. She sits on the beach and looks at the blue sea and thinks about ... well, *you* know.

But Monty doesn't know. "What's the matter with Jenny?" he thinks. "Why is she unhappy? Why doesn't she play cricket with me and the others?" He wags his tail and barks. Then he licks Jenny's face. That's nice, isn't it? But Jenny says, "Oh, Monty, go away. Leave me alone."

She listens to a sad song on Toby's walkman. Then she gets up and goes to the harbour. She looks at the ships and boats. But it's no fun without ... *you* know who. Jenny buys some letter paper at a shop. Then she goes to a snack bar. "A cup of tea, please," she says. She takes out the paper and her pen:

"Dear Dennis ..."

15 *to lick* lecken

Jenny's dog – Exercises, games, ideas

One

The Jacobs family

a) Toby is Jenny's ________________________.

b) Mrs Jacobs is Toby's and Jenny's ________________________.

c) Jenny is Toby's ________________________.

d) Mr Jacobs is Jenny's and Toby's ________________________.

e) Monty is Jenny's ________________________.

f) The Jacobses live in ________________________.

Two

What's right? (√)

1. ☐ Mrs Jacobs takes Jenny to the kennels.
   ☐ Mr Jacobs takes Bradbury to the kennels.
   ☐ Mrs Jacobs takes Monty to the kennels.
2. ☐ The Jacobses can't take Monty to Germany.
   ☐ Monty doesn't want to go to Germany.
   ☐ Monty wants to go to the kennels.
3. ☐ They have rabies in England.
   ☐ We have rabies in Germany.

Three

A crossword puzzle

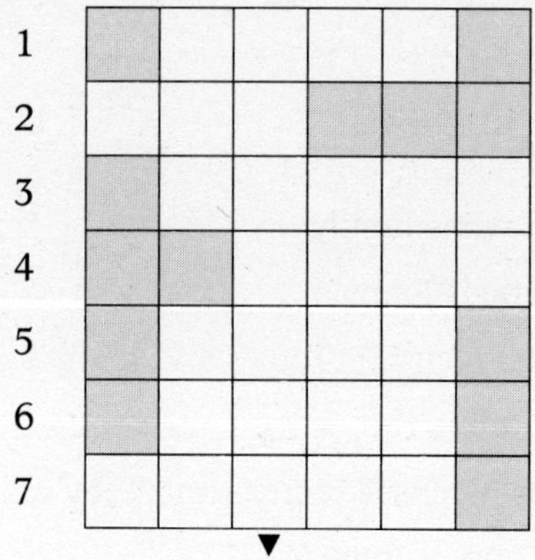

Rostock has got a big ____________.

1. A big boat.
2. You can swim in it.
3. 
4. 
5. Jenny leaves it in the car.
6. A town in England.
7. It takes cars from Britain to Holland.

Four

Poor Monty! *Find the right words.*

Monty is . . .
happy, alone, red, asleep, angry, hungry, blue, cold, funny, ill, afraid, lucky

Five

Right (r) or wrong (w)?

1. Jenny wants to go to Bradbury. ☐
2. Jenny walks to Bradbury. ☐
3. Max takes Jenny to York in his truck. ☐
4. Max is a bus driver. ☐
5. Linda is a cowboy. ☐
6. Linda is going to Newcastle. ☐
7. Linda can take Jenny to Bradbury. ☐

Six

On the car ferry. *Write a dialogue, like this:*

Mr Jacobs: Stop the boat! We want to go back to England.
Captain: Why? Don't you like my ship?
Mrs Jacobs: …
Captain: …
Toby: …
…

You can read or act the dialogue in groups of four.

Eight

Linda

1. Linda is a ________________ ________________.
2. She wears ________________ and ________________.
3. She likes ________________ music.

Nine/Ten

Trick nineteen

Fill in the map.

One to Eleven

Who do you like?

Mr Jacobs	
Mrs Jacobs	
Toby	
Jenny	
Monty	
The Captain	
Max	
Linda	
Mrs Taylor	
Sam	
Brian	
Fred	
Queenie	

I don't like him/her. = –

I like him/her. = +

He/she is great! = ++

What do the other boys and girls in your class think?

Two dogs at the seaside – Exercises, games, ideas

One

Easy cricket for the beach

wicket bat ball

Players: 2 – ?
Two teams
Team A (batting team)
Team B (bowling team)

Rules

1. A player from team B throws the ball ("bowls").
2. If the ball hits the wicket, the player from team A is "out". Then it's the next player's turn. When all the players of team A are "out", it's team B's turn to bat.
3. When the "batter" hits the ball, he or she can run. Each "run" (= 10 metres) is one point.
4. The batter is "out" if
   - a player from the bowling team catches the ball before it hits the ground;
   - a player from the bowling team hits the wicket with the ball when the batter is running between ① and ②;
   - the "bowler" hits the wicket with the ball.
5. The team which has the most runs wins.

①
10 metres
②

Two

Do you like steak?
What do you like to eat and drink?

Give points *(Punkte)*, like this:

I like … a lot 2 points	I like … 1 point	I don't like … 0 points
	cornflakes	cheese

steak, chips
hamburgers, sausages
bacon, eggs

apples, oranges, bananas

cornflakes, yoghurt

bread and butter, rolls,
sandwiches, toast
cheese, marmalade

tea, coffee, milk,
lemonade, coke

biscuits, cake, chocolate, sweets

Four/five

On the moors. *Put the sentences in the right order:*
A) Monty looks for Toby and Queenie.
B) But it's no fun without Toby.
C) Queenie runs away.
D) Toby walks for a long time.
E) It's Queenie. She is barking.
F) And she's too heavy for Toby.
G) Dennis, Jenny and Monty hear something.
H) Toby tells Queenie, "Get help."
I) Then he hears a voice far away.
J) Dennis and Jenny visit Whitby harbour.
K) It's Mrs Owen.
The first sentence is (D) . . .

Seven

Mr Blunt. *Write a dialogue, like this:*
Mrs Jacobs: Well, we must call the police.
Mr Jacobs: Oh no, not again!
Mr Blunt (on the telephone): Yes . . . Yes, that's right . . .
. . .
You can read or act the dialogue in groups of five: Mr and Mrs Jacobs, Mr Blunt, a policeman – and Queenie . . .

Ten

Dear Dennis . . .
Can you write Jenny's letter? Your teacher can help you. Or you can take the best words and sentences from new or old pop songs and put them together . . .

European Language Institute

YOUR ENGLISH MONTHLY

Sprachzeitschriften

Für Schülerinnen und Schüler mit ca. 2-3 Lernjahren Englisch

Klett-Nr. 97321

Für Schülerinnen und Schüler mit ca. 4 Lernjahren Englisch

Klett-Nr. 97323

Sprachzeitschriften

Zu abonnieren bei:
Ernst Klett Schulbuchverlag
Postfach 1170
71398 Korb